ŠEVČÍK
Op. 1 Part 2

SCHOOL OF TECHNIQUE

SCHULE DER TECHNIK

ÉCOLE DE TECHNIQUE

for

VIOLA

(ALTO)

arranged / bearbeitet / arrangées

by   von   par

Lionel Tertis

Italian viola by Pietro Giovanni Mantegazza, c. 1780,
with kind permission of Christie's, London.

Bosworth

REMEMBER!

(1) The first consideration in string playing, is the attainment of *perfect intonation*. This can only be achieved by the most *intense* and *concentrated* listening, (not superficial listening). *Never* pass a note that is the slightest degree out of tune.

(2) *Hold* and *keep* your fingers down on the strings in all these exercises, whenever and wherever it is at all possible.

(3) Attention must be paid to accurate note *values*. Be particularly careful when there are two notes with *separate* bows, immediately followed by two notes of the same value in one bow, or one note separately, followed by three notes of the same value in one bow etc. etc. No matter how varied the groupings, every note must be of exact equal value.

(4) When practising these exercises *slowly* lift your fingers high and feel you are doing so from the *knuckles* and bring your fingers down hard on the fingerboard,—when practising them *rapidly*, do not lift your fingers high and put them down *lightly* on the fingerboard.

(5) Divide the bowing up so as to, *first,* practise the exercises slowly and play them in tune. When you can do this efficiently, use the bowing as indicated, or as many notes in the one bow as possible.

NOTICE

(1) La première qualité qu'il faut s'appliquer à obtenir, lors de l'étude de tout instrument à cordes, est la *justesse d'intonation*. Celle-ci ne s'acquiert qu'au prix d'une attention *soutenue* et *concentrée* (pas d'attention superficielle). Veillez donc à ce que chaque note soit rigoureusement juste sans faire la plus minime concession à la médiocrité.

(2) Au cours de ces exercices *posez* et *maintenez* les doigts bien appuyés sur les cordes partout où la chose est possible.

(3) Observez minutieusement la *valeur* des notes. Veillez y spécialement lorsque deux notes avec coups d'archet *séparés* se trouvent être suivies de deux autres notes de même valeur mais figurant dans un même coup d'archet, ou lorsqu'une note isolée est suivie de trois notes de même valeur dans un même coup d'archet, etc.. Les diverses façons dont les notes peuvent être groupées importent peu, pourvu qu'à chacune d'elles il soit toujours donné sa valeur adéquate.

(4) Commencez par jouer ces exercices *au ralenti* et faites en sorte que les doigts s'élèvent très haut. Il faut vraiment sentir que tout le travail se fait dans les charnières des *articulations*. Abaissez ensuite avec force les doigts sur le manche. Lorsque, par la suite, vous jouez ces exercices en un tempo plus *accéléré,* levez les doigts moins haut et abaissez les sur le manche avec plus de légèreté.

(5) Répartissez vos coups d'archet de manière à jouer d'abord ces exercices en un tempo assez lent mais toujours avec une intonation rigoureusement juste. Dès que vous serez à même de jouer de la sorte avec aisance, accélérez et conformez-vous aux indications des coups d'archet tout en vous appliquant à jouer le plus de notes possibles en un seul coup d'archet.

ZUR BEACHTUNG

(1) Von vordringlicher Wichtigkeit für das Spielen auf Streichinstrumenten ist *untadelig-saubere Intonation*. Diese kann nur erreicht werden durch intensiv-konzentriertes (niemals oberflächliches) *Hören*. Lass keinen Ton durchgehen, der auch nur im geringsten unrein in der Stimmung ist.

(2) Lass bei diesen Übungen die *Finger auf der Saite liegen,* soweit und solange es möglich ist.

(3) Achte auf genaue *Notenwerte*, besonders wenn auf zwei *einzeln gestrichene* Noten unmittelbar zwei *gebundene* Noten gleichen Wertes folgen— oder auf eine einzeln gestrichene Note drei gebundene gleichen Wertes usw. Ganz gleichgültig, wie die Notengruppen auf den Bogen verteilt sind: Stets muss jede Note genau den ihr zugehörigen Wert erhalten.

(4) Beim *langsamen* Üben die Finger hoch (aus dem Knöchelgelenk) aufheben und energisch auf das Griffbrett aufsetzen—beim *schnellen* Üben nur wenig aufheben und locker aufsetzen.

(5) Studiere die Übungen *zuerst langsam* mit sauberer, schöner Tongebung, dann erst halte dich an die angegebenen Bögen oder spiele auf einen Bogen so viel Noten wie möglich.

B. & Co.Ltd.21508b

SEVCIK. Op. 1 — Viola (Alto)

DEUXIEME PARTIE
Exercices à la 2e Position
On travaillera chaque exercice en détaché et en lié.

SECOND PART
Exercises in the 2nd Position
Each to be practised staccato and legato.

ZWEITER TEIL
Übungen in der 2ten Lage
Man übe jedes Beispiel gestossen und gebunden.

1

Played thus:
Exécution:
Ausführung:

21508b

2

Chaque fois que vous rencontrez un unisson, assurez-vous si celui-ci sonne rigoureusement juste. Si tel n'est pas le cas, c'est un signe que la justesse des notes qui le précèdent laissait à désirer.

Note that the unisons are perfectly in tune when you arrive at them, if they are not, then your fault lies before them.

Achte auf vollkommene Reinheit des Primen-Einklangs (mit den blanken Saiten). Erklingen sie unrein, dann war bestimmt die Intonation der vorangegangenen Doppelgriffe bereits ungenügend.

3

Maintenez vos deux doigts abaissés pour chaque octave.

Keep the 2 fingers down for each octave.

Setze für jede Oktave beide Finger zugleich auf.

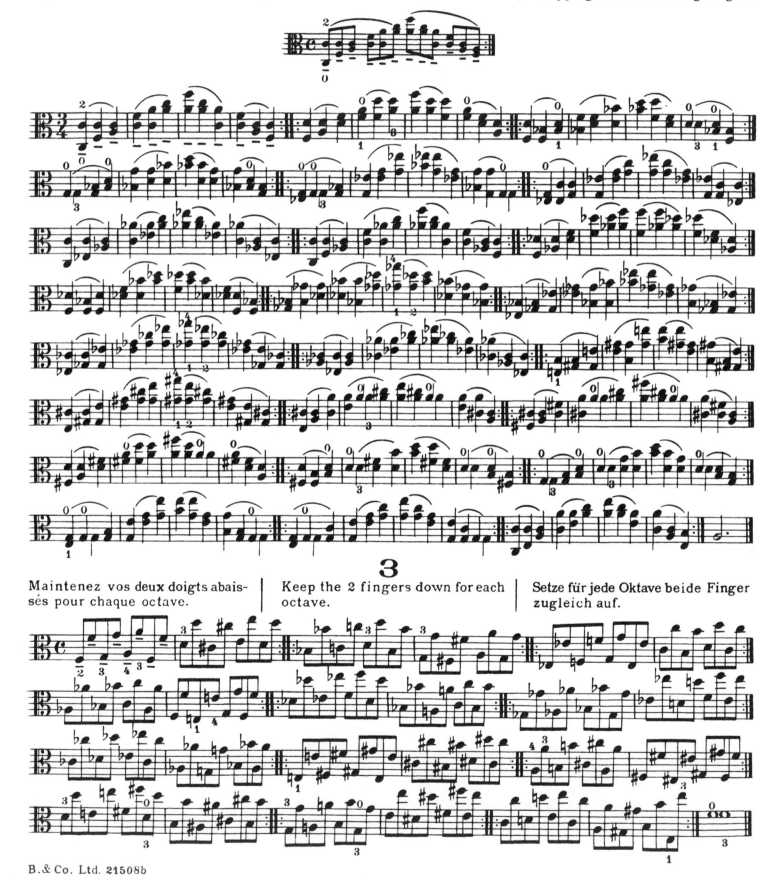

B.& Co. Ltd. 21508b

4

Exercises in the
1st and 2nd Positions
The actual change of position must be done quickly. Endeavour to make the change without accent or jerk and with as little trace of portamento as possible.

Übungen in der
1ten und 2ten Lage
Der Lagenwechsel muss rasch, ohne Ruck oder Akzent, mit nur einer Spur portamento (Gleiten) erfolgen.

5

N'oubliez pas le discret porta-mento. (Pas de hiatus) | Don't forget– discreet porta-mento. (no scooping!) | Beachte: Diskretes portamento. (ohne Krampf!)

6

Accord de septième diminuée	Chord of the Diminished seventh	Verminderter Septimenakkord
Tenez les rondes sans les jouer.	Hold down the semibreves (whole notes) without sounding them.	Die ganzen Noten sind zu greifen ohne gespielt zu werden.

7

Exercices dans tous le tons | *Exercises in all keys* | *Übungen in allen Tonarten*

Étudiez ces exercices également en coups d'archet séparés | Practise this exercise in separate bowings also | Übe diese Beispiele auch in getrennten Bogenstrichen.

B. & Co. Ltd. 21508b

*)8

Divers accords arpégés   *Various arpeggiated chords*   *Verschiedene Akkorde arpeggiert*

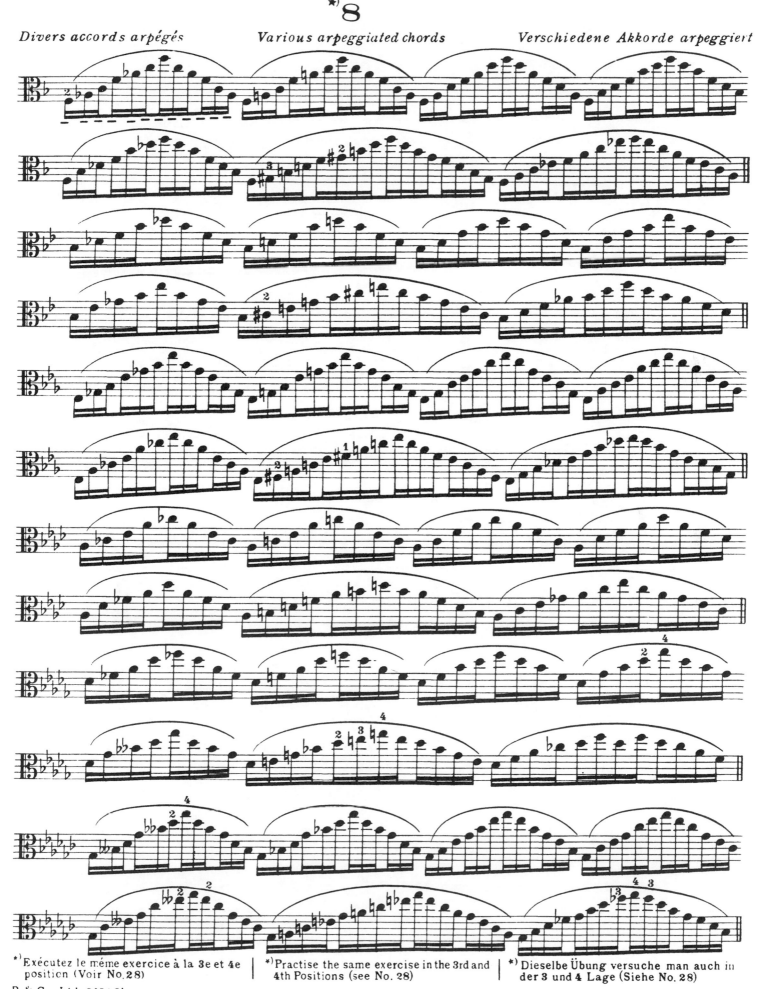

*)Exécutez le méme exercice à la 3e et 4e position (Voir No. 28) │ *)Practise the same exercise in the 3rd and 4th Positions (see No. 28) │ *)Dieselbe Übung versuche man auch in der 3 und 4 Lage (Siehe No. 28)

B.& Co. Ltd. 21508b

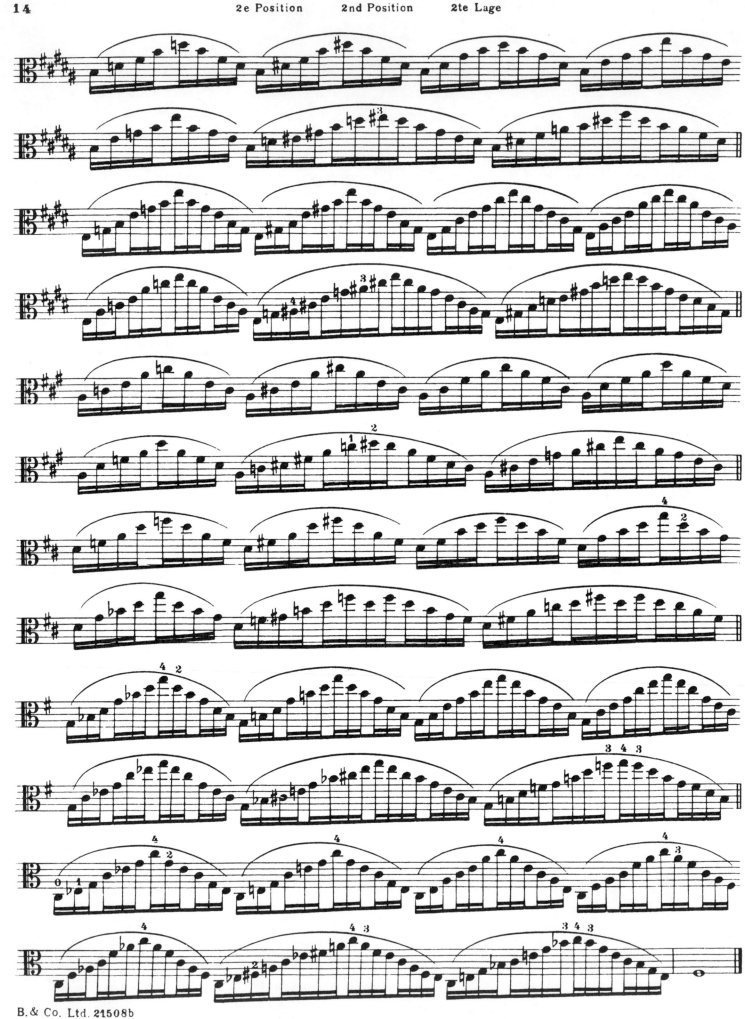

B. & Co. Ltd. 21508b

9

Gamme chromatique | *Chromatic Scales* | *Chromatische Tonleiter*

B. & Co. Ltd. 21508b

2e Position   2nd Position   2te Lage

10

Exercices en doubles notes
dans tous les tons

Surveillez l'intonation.

Exercises in double stopping
in all the keys

Take care of your intonation

Übungen in Doppelgriffen
in allen Tonarten

Achte sorgfältig auf die Intonation!

b. & Co. Ltd. 21508b

11

Exercices á la 3me Position

(Rappel) Il faut que la ronde reste tenue dans le ton aussi bien que la noire.

Exercises in the 3rd Position

(To remind) The holding down semibreve must be kept and played in tune as well as the crotchet.

Übungen in der 3ten Lage

(Zur Erinnerung:) Achte auf tonliche Übereinstimmung der durchgehaltenen ganzen Noten mit den Vierteln!

12

Maintenez le 1r doigt abaissé tout au long de cet exercice (même si la chose nécessite une certaine contorsion de la main) et veillez constamment à la justesse du son.

Keep 1st finger down all through this exercise (even when you have to shift it) and frequently check it to see if it is in tune.

Lass den 1. Finger (auch nach seiner Erhöhung oder Erniedrigung) die ganze Übung hindurch liegen, überprüfe häufig die Richtigkeit seiner Tonhöhe.

13

Essayez *aussi* de jouer cet exercice piano. Lorsque vous le jouez forte, tâchez de ne point *forcer* la sonorité.

Try *also* to play this exercise piano. When playing this exercise forte avoid accents or *forcing* of tone.

Versuche die Übung *ebenso* piano zu spielen. Vermeide, wenn du die Übung forte spielst, Akzente und *Forcierung* des Tones.

(Le même son durant *tout* le coup d'archet)

(even tone *whole* length of bow)

(gleichmässig = ruhiger Ton über die *ganze* Bogenlänge).

B.& Co. Ltd. 21508b

14

Laissez les doigts sur les cordes aussi longtemps que possible.	Hold the fingers down on the strings as long as possible.	Die Finger sind so lange als möglich liegen zu lassen.

15

Exercices à la 1re et 3e Position

Efforcez-vous à ne pas laisser paraître les differents changements de position. Rèduisez les portamenti au strict minimum. Surtout pas de heurts aux changements de position.

Exercises in the 1st and 3rd Positions

Conceal the changes of position as much as possible, reduce Portamento to absolute minimum- no jerks in changing positions.

Übungen in der 1ten und 3ten Lage

Der Lagenwechsel muss kaum hörbar, ohne jeden Ruck oder Stoss erfolgen. Reduziere das portamento auf ein Minimum.

2e et 3e Position | *2nd and 3rd Position* | *2te und 3te Lage*

B. & Co. Ltd. 21508b

16

| Tenez les rondes sans les jouer | Hold down the semibreves (whole notes) without sounding them. | Die ganzen Noten sind zu greifen, ohne gespielt zu werden. |

17

18

19

Exercices à la 4me Position | *Exercises in the 4th Position* | *Übungen in der 4ten Lage*

20

| Allez-y bien posément pas de saccades | Practise slowly, watch Intonation! | Übe langsam, achte auf die Intonation! |

21

| Maintenez les doigts sur les cordes aussi longtemps que possible. | Keep fingers on strings as long as possible. | Lass die Finger so lange als möglich liegen. |

22

| Exercices à la 1re et 4e Positions Portamento discret! Pas de heurts! | Exercises in the 1st and 4th Positions Discreet Portamento! no jerks! | Übungen in der 1ten und 4ten Lage Diskretes portamento! Keinen Ruck beim Lagenwechsel! |

B. & Co. Ltd. 21508b

23

Exercices à la 2e et 4e Position | *Exercises in the 2nd and 4th Positions* | *Übungen in der 2ten und 4ten Lage*

24

25

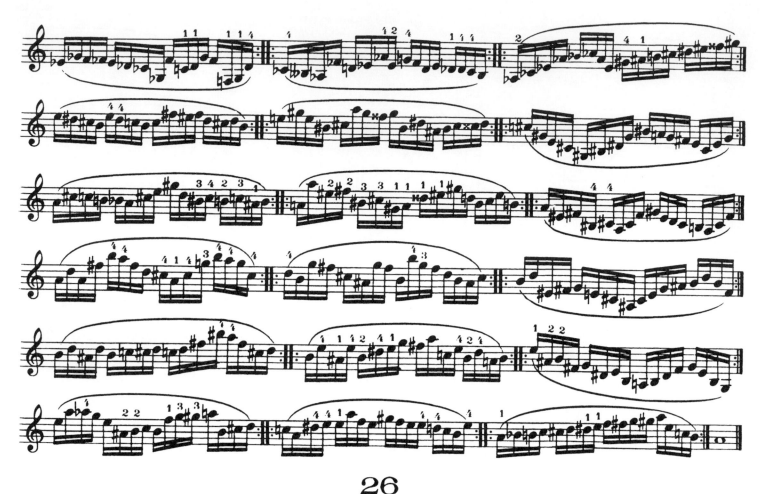

26

Exercices à la 5me Position | *Exercises in the 5th Position* | *Übungen in der 5ten Lage*

28

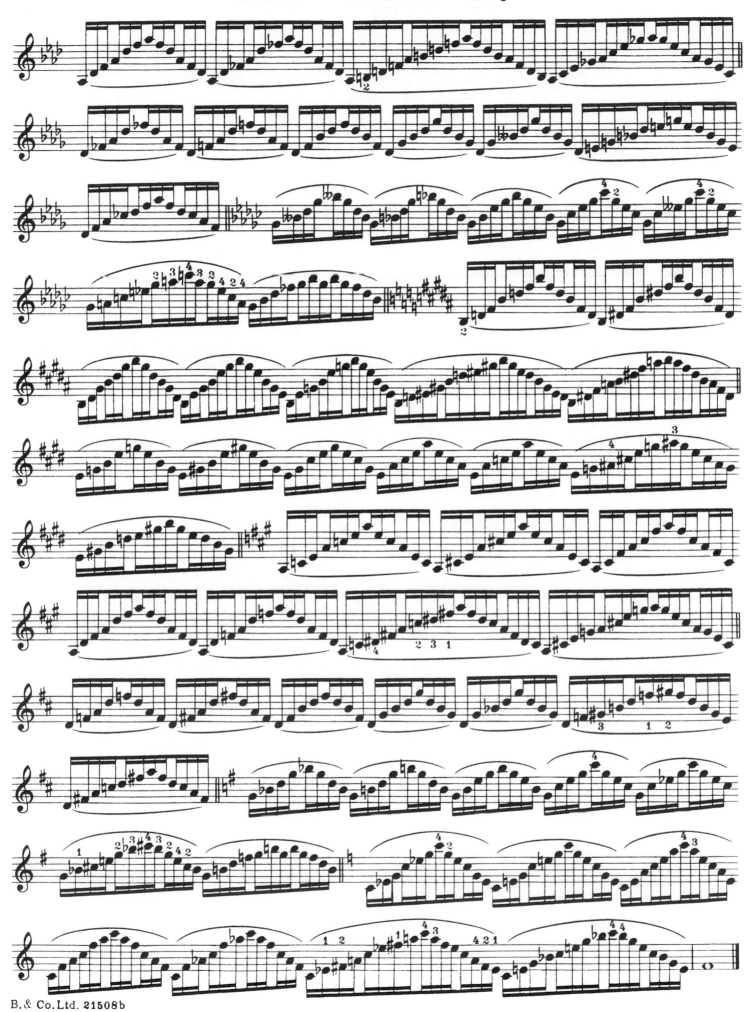

29

Exercices à la 6me Position
Maintenez le 1r doigt abaissé
aussi longtemps que possible.
N'oubliez pas, lorsque vous jouez
lentement, de lever les doigts
aussi haut que possible en fai-
sant jouer les articulations.

Exercises in the 6th Position
Keep your first finger down
wherever possible. Don't for-
get when practising slowly
to lift your fingers high from
the knuckles.

Übungen in der 6ten Lage
1. Finger liegen lassen, wo im-
mer es möglich ist. Vergiss
beim langsamen Üben nicht, die
Finger (aus dem Knöchelgelenk)
hoch aufzuheben.

30

31

| *Exercices à la 7me Position* | *Exercises in the 7th Position* | *Übungen in der 7ten Lage* |
| Le 1r doigt abaissé | 1st finger down | 1. Finger liegen lassen |

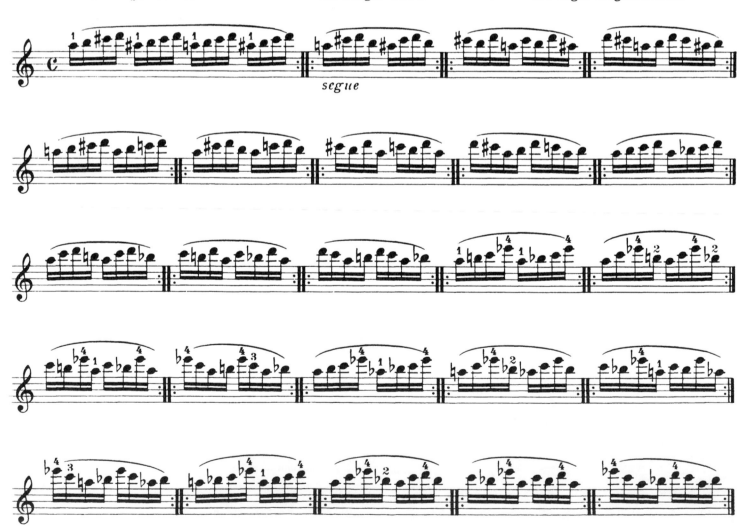

PUBLISHERS OF MUSIC FOR THE SERIOUS VIOLIST

Studies

ARNOLD, Alan
3-Octave Scales & Arpeggios
BLUMENSTENGAL, A.
Viola Scale Technique Bk.1 - 1st Pos.
Viola Scale Technique Bk.2 -1-5 Pos.
HOFMANN, Richard
Melodic Double-Stop Studies Op. 96
TARTINI, Giuseppe
The Art of Bowing

Viola Solo

ARNOLD, Alan
Cadenzas for Telemann Viola Concerto
KREISLER, Fritz
Recitative and Scherzo Caprice
WOEHR, Christian
Bachiana

Viola & Piano Albums

ARNOLD, Alan
The Young Violist Bk. 1 (easy pieces)
The Young Violist Bk. 2 (more pieces)
BACH, J.S.
Basic Bach (arr.Arnold)
BEETHOVEN, Ludwig van
Beethoven's Best (arr. Arnold)
MOZART, W.A
Mozart Miniatures (arr. Arnold)

Viola & Piano Repertoire

BACH, J.S.
Bourrée in C minor
Chromatic Fantasy and Fugue
BEETHOVEN, Ludwig van
Für Elise
BENJAMIN, Arthur
Jamaican Rumba
BOCCHERINI, Luigi
Music Box Minuet
BÖHM, Carl
Sarabande
BOROWSKI, Felix
Adoration
BRAHMS, Johannes
Scherzo
CHOPIN, Frédéric
Nocturne
CORELLI, Arcangelo
Sarabande, Giga and Badinerie
Sonata No.12 - La Folia con
Variazione

DANCLA, Charles
Carnival of Venice
DE BÉRIOT, Ch.
Scène de Ballet
DEBUSSY, Claude
Girl with the Flaxen Hair
La Plus Que Lente
DVORÁK, Antonin
Romance Op. 11
Sonatina Op. 100
FAURÉ, Gabriel
Fantasie
FIOCCO, Gioseffo-Hectore
Allegro
FRANCOEUR, François
Sonata in A
GLUCK, Christoff W. von
Melody from *Orfeo ed Euridice*
HANDEL, G.F.
Bourrée
Concerto in B flat
Sonata in B flat
Sonata in D
HUBAY, Jenö
Hejre Kati
JENKINSON, Ezra
Elves' Dance (*Elfentanz*)
JOPLIN, Scott
Pineapple Rag
Solace
KREISLER, Fritz
Liebesfreud
Liebesleid
Praeludium and Allegro
Sicilienne and Rigaudon
MASSENET, Jules
Meditation from *Thaïs*
MATTHEWS, Holon
Fantasy
MENDELSSOHN, Felix
Sonata in E flat
MOZART, W.A.
Adagio K.261
Menuetto Divertimento K.334
Rondo K.250
Serenata Cantabile
MUSSORGSKY, Modest
Hopak
NOVACEK, Ottokar
Perpetual Motion
PAGANINI, Niccolò
Six Sonatas Bk. 1, Nos 1, 2,3
Six Sonatas Bk. 2, Nos 4, 5, 6
Variations on the G-String
PUGNANI, Gaetano
Gavotta Variata

RACHMANINOFF, Sergei
Vocalise
RIES, Franz
Perpetuum Mobile
RIMSKY-KORSAKOV, N.
Flight of the Bumble Bee
SCHMIDT, Ernst
Alla Turca
SHUBERT, Franz
The Bee
TARTINI, Giuseppe
Sonata angelique
The Devil's Trill
TCHAIKOVSKY, P.
Canzonetta
June Barcarolle
Mélodie
Sérénade mélancholique
Valse sentimentale
VITALI, Giovanni
Chaconne
VIVALDI, Antonio
Sonata in G
WEBER, Carl M.
Andante and Hungarian Rondo
WIENIAWSKI, Henryk
Légende
Scherzo Tarantella

Viola Duos

BACH, J. S.
Fifteen Two-Part Inventions
MOZART, W.A.
Duo Sonata in B flat K.292
Twelve Duets K.487

3 Violas & Piano

PACHELBEL, Johann
Canon

4 Violas

TELEMANN, Georg Philipp
Concerto No. 1 in C for 4 Violas
Concerto No. 2 in G for 4 Violas
Concerto No. 3 in F for 4 Violas
Concerto No. 4 in D for 4 Violas

4 Violas & Piano

VIVALDI, Antonio
Concerto for 4 Violas and Piano

Available from:

Bosworth